Being
PROACTIVE
is the Key!

20 ESSENTIAL TIPS TO
BECOME AN EFFECTIVE PARTNER WITH YOUR
CHILD'S SCHOOL AND SET THEM UP FOR SUCCESS!

Nichole Renee

Speaker, Consultant & Author
Nichole Renee Enterprises

This book is full of tips to get your teen a great head start, keep money in your pocket and get them closer to the college of their dreams! Blessings!

Nichole Renee

Nichole Renee
Abington, PA

Disclaimer
The purpose of this book is to educate and entertain. The author and/or publisher do not guarantee that anyone following these techniques, suggestions, tips, ideas, or strategies will become successful. The author and/or publisher shall have neither liability nor responsibility to anyone with respect to any loss of damage caused, or alleged to be caused, directly or indirectly by the information contained in this book.

Editing: Meredith Pileggi and Robin Devonish
Front Cover: pro_ebookcovers via Fiverr
Back Cover/Interior: Nichole Renee

ISBN 13: 978-0-9981919-2-8
Printed in the United States of America

In my twenty+ year career as an educator, I have advised more than 1,000 students and parents in the areas of self-esteem, motivation, accountability, and college/career planning.

School climates are ever-changing, and you need an ally to guide you through the many issues and concerns that affect your child in relation to post-high school planning.

Nichole Renee Enterprises™ (NRE) Virtual School Counseling program offers cutting-edge services beyond the traditional college consulting programs. NRE uses a data-driven approach to get information about your child's social and academic history. We perform "status checks" to set your child up for success by constructing a plan that gives your child a competitive advantage.

Partner with us today and build confidence as you receive the best tools and support to identify the appropriate post-graduation options for your son or daughter.

www.NicholeReneeEnterprises.com

Dedication

This book is dedicated to Ebony McDuffie and Alicia Anderson. Who knew that a random summer job search in 1995 would change my life forever! You and the other enthusiastic girls in that 5th grade class at the North Philadelphia Freedom School introduced me to the field of education. Through your curiosity and zest for learning, I was able to experience first-hand how inequity and politics undermine the efforts of under-served youth on a daily basis. Moreover, I recognized the importance of programs such as the Freedom School to exist and act as a safe haven for children. Because of that experience, I changed my career course from clinical psychology to school counseling.

Because of you, 21 years later I am still inspired to do this work, fighting to even the playing field for the underdog. I love you both and am honored to still be a part of your lives today.

Acknowledgements

With deep-felt gratitude, I acknowledge my parents Fred & Valerie Johnson for being symbols of integrity, professionalism, and character. You taught and modeled the importance of the pursuit of education, good citizenship, and the importance of family and friends. Thank you for always being available to listen to all of my ideas--no matter how crazy the venture. I love you both!

Corrie and Rissa for allowing me to see what it's like as a parent on the opposite side of the table.

My sister and best friend Anita Betole for critiquing everything that I write and giving me your honest and quirky opinion—even regarding my love for commas. Although you are the little sister, there have been many times that you stop your world to help me. Please know that I appreciate it and will let Jesus know to put your seat that much closer to the gates of heaven so you have a better view of who's coming in.

My long-time partners-in-crime, Sharon Sadler and Donetta McQueen. You've been here for the good, the bad and the ugly. That is all behind us now and I am racing you both to the top.

Reverend Geneva A. Hackett for mentoring me for years, particularly through that rough patch a few years back. You assured me I would land on top. That "table" I've been preparing is set—"you understand."

My fellow school counselors, colleagues, and friends in the world of education (especially the crazy counselors at Norristown Area High School and everyone in the Philadelphia College Prep Roundtable)—you rock!

Salome Thomas-El for serving as a model for people whose calling is to stay in the schools, and at the same time, pursue their dreams to serve children outside of the school day. "I Choose to Stay" as well.

Darrell "Coach D" Andrews for being the first person to actually challenge me to write a book. I looked at you like you were crazy, but now I understand.

Sheri Luckey and Johnna Ithier for cramping in that booth for hours at Ruby Tuesday after that long workshop to "mastermind" about the books we were going to write.

Those zany ladies of the *Damsels In Success* for giving me the privilege of "sharpening my saw" with you over the last 2 years. Thank you Andrea "Diva" Lawful-Sanders for seeing something in me and adding me to the family. Loraine Ballard Morrill, much love for that iHeart interview. Lu Ann Cahn for "daring" that group of ladies on that chilly Sunday to do something different. Little did I know this book would be one of the many new dares I did this year.

For anyone else I missed, I'll catch you on the next book!

Special Thanks

Anita Betole, Sharon Sadler, Rodchine Lusane, Danielle Lewis, Melonie Butler and Donetta McQueen for providing feedback about this book and all other life matters. You guys keep me grounded and laughing…all...the...time!

Robin "The Self-Publishing Maven" Devonish for guiding me through every facet of my first two books.

Meredith Pileggi, your perspective as a teacher added more depth to this book. You were my clutch player in the 23rd hour and I am extremely grateful. You saved more than the day!

Prologue

Growing up as a 70's kid in the south was an interesting experience. It was a time where the community was still allowed to help raise and discipline kids. There were no personal computers or cell phones, but parents seemed to quickly find out what their children were doing inside and outside of school.

For me, sixth grade was the worst. My homeroom teacher, Mr. McCray, was my mother's friend, so she had a direct line to the intel. Who needed social media when Mr. McCray provided the daily scoop? Every morning, I would see him and just roll my eyes.

He was the ultimate snitch!

My parents were all up in my business. They were actively involved in the Parent Teacher Association (PTA), parent conferences, and pretty much anything important that was going on at school. They knew when the report cards were coming and when we had early dismissals. They were letting me know I needed to be on my A-game and, in their words, "act like I had some sense."

They were sooo annoying!

What I didn't realize at the time was that they were branding our family. They were letting the school know I had parents who cared. They were letting the school know they couldn't create or enforce a policy that didn't support me, as a person and future contributor to society. They were making themselves known.

As an adult and parent, I get it now. Mr. McCray still gets a serious eye-roll though.

TABLE OF CONTENTS

Introduction

Day in and day out, I talk to overstressed parents frustrated with how to get their teen graduated on time, on to college, all while finding the money to pay for it. Many find themselves scrambling at the 12th hour in the days leading up to the big move on campus. This college campus is where their child will spend the next four years of their life and the parent(s) want to ensure that everything is properly put in place:

What are these new forms and summer deadlines that we need to meet? Should we buy or rent books? Which meal plan should we choose? Who is the weird roommate you are paired with? How do we get more money for school?

The stress is real!

During the time I was a parent going through the high school years, I was right there with the parents mentioned above. I was married and raising two girls while maintaining a full-time job as a school counselor. I also had a side business and was a very active volunteer at my church. I know how it feels to have all of those balls in the air while trying to stay on top of everyone's schedules, activities and deadlines. I had the same stressors that you have. To add, there are several stressors regarding how to fund college for our children. We leave a lot of money on the table that could have gone towards tuition or kept in our pockets if we had planned more strategically.

It's all about planning.

Think about it - When a person becomes "famous" it doesn't "just happen." If someone wants to have solid success, some foundational steps were taken over a period of years to get to that magical moment.

You hear about award-winning producers that started out hanging up flyers in the neighborhood or working their way up from the mailroom. You hear about Olympic gold medalists that started training at the age of eight, working for hours every day, while looking for the right coach, nutritionist, and agent to get them to "that moment." You hear about the path that the President of the United States has to walk, run, or crawl to become the leader of the free world.

Preparing for post-secondary goals is no different.

Author Steven Covey, in his book *The 7 Habits of Highly Effective People*, discusses his concept "beginning with the end in mind." In his concept, you must to look at the final result you desire and plan backward to see it to fruition.

The goal of this book is to provide you with information and tools to help you effectively maneuver through the complicated school system.

This book is written from the perspective of an educator in the system, discussing the typical issues and concerns the school solves for parents. It's my desire to equip you with the tools necessary in gaining a competitive edge in order to take full advantage of all available options, so that you can be proactive and not reactive.

This book contains information and terms related to any programs and/or special services to where your child should have access and is divided into three sections:

* Getting involved, being engaged, and knowing your rights
* Parenting skills and making use of special services
* Strategies to effectively plan for college

Part I
Getting Involved, Being Engaged, and Knowing Your Rights

The most important thing that a parent can do to help their student is get involved in their school. Studies continue to show that parents who are actively involved in their child's education yield long-lasting and positive results. Sometimes being involved is easier said than done! Your life is busy, drenched with the many hats you wear: putting out fires, keeping up with one or more of your loved ones' schedules—and what does being "involved" mean?

Tip #1
Be Proactive and
Intervene Early

"The most important role models should and could be parents and teachers. But that said, once you're a teenager you've probably gotten as much of an example from your parents as you're going to."

-Andrew Shue-

Parents and students typically wait until the junior or senior year of high school to begin planning for college.

This is too late!

Yes, it's true that senior year is technically the beginning of the application process. But the true beginning lies in the early stages of middle and high school. Planning during these years will prepare your child to take the appropriate courses and receive the best options regarding scholarships and college placement. If you wait until the last minute, you can't go backward to try to fix mistakes.

By senior year, your child is finishing up their required classes and their transcript (a record of all high school courses and standardized tests) is set. Most of the extra-curricular activities would be complete, and summer programs would be over.

So where do you start?

The key things parents should do at any grade level are:

* Get involved by attending teacher conferences, open houses, sporting events, or Parent Teacher Association (PTA) meetings. Ensuring visibility is a primary way to communicate that you are an advocate for your child and their future.

* Communicate regularly via phone, email, or in person with teachers. Make the teacher the primary contact.

* Check grades, attendance, and discipline regularly, whether online or by school contact.

* Plan a school success routine (getting adequate sleep, prepping clothes and a school bag at night, and checking homework completion).

* Work with the school staff as a team member (i.e. attending meetings, holding each other accountable, etc.).

* Volunteer in your child's classroom, chaperone field trips, or have lunch at school (elementary or middle school; high schools don't typically allow this).

Opportunities for parental involvement can become sparse at the high school level. More independence and autonomy is given to adolescents with the expectation of developing a sense of personal responsibility. And as they become more responsible for themselves, the need or desire for parental guidance begins to be weaned out.

Tip #2
Be Engaged and Aware

Ask your child about their day, and don't accept "It was cool" as an answer. In several cases, there are new learning and teaching methods of which we have no clue (like the 'new' math). Being honest, it is okay to admit you don't remember some, if not a lot, of the content! It doesn't matter if you know how to write five paragraph literary analyses or balance equations, but simply by asking your child how school is going is a great indicator as to whether or not they understand what they are doing.

Access is easy!

Everything is now electronic and easier for you to gain access. Check grades, attendance, behavior, schedules, and teacher emails. Go online every week and scroll through the grades. Look to see that there are no zeros, tardiness, absences, or class cuts. Learning cannot take place if a student is consistently out of the classroom.

There are plenty of parents who are surprised at the end of the year regarding their son or daughter's grades and attendance. If you are keeping track of the elements of your child's performance that help to determine the ease with which they will transition out of school, there should not be any big surprises. Many parents believe it is the responsibility of the teacher to make them aware of issues. This is true. It is also the job of the parent to be proactive and reach out as well. At the end of the day, this is your child.

Be warned, at the high school level, your child will openly despise you getting involved in their affairs (except for when they want you to "stick it" to a teacher who they feel wronged them). However, as much as it annoys them, underneath the fight, they secretly appreciate the fact that you're showing interest.

Tip #3
Learn to Build Relationships and Brand Your Family

One of the best-kept secrets to set your child up for success, just like anything in life, is not what you know but who you know. Every personal contact, phone call, and email sets the stage for the school to learn about your family. You want to put yourself in a position to build positive and fruitful relationships with the school staff.

Periodic check-ins with the school are essential, especially at the beginning of the year. These opportunities allow you to meet the teachers, principal, and critical staff as well as develop a truer sense of the people with whom your child will work with on a daily basis. Make it a point to go to the school and introduce yourself. Call or make an appointment with the school counselor or designee. Check them out, share a little bit about yourself, and discuss any questions or concerns you may have.

These simple actions send a strong message to the school that you are a concerned parent, and you strive to be proactive in your child's education. The school staff appreciates it, and it will give them that much more motivation to go out of their way for your son/daughter.

Of course, your level of involvement with the school depends on your child's needs. For instance, if your child maintains good grades, good behavior, and is involved in activities, your involvement can be minimal to moderate, but consistent. If your child struggles with grades, behavior, or has needs that require more assistance, (special education, medical concerns, mental health concerns, etc.) then it is essential that you be more involved.

Make yourself known without becoming "that" parent.

On many occasions, parents only go to the school when either something terrible or great happens. Everyone wants school to be great all the time, but logically we know things can't always be perfect. There will be situations that will shake you—especially when you feel the school has done "your baby" wrong. You want to storm through the building like the Tasmanian Devil to tear the place up, and you want them to know you mean business.

In my experience, there are parents who habitually enter in that way and, most of the time, get what they want. Their reputations make the school cringe at the thought of them emailing, calling, or coming in. Subconsciously, it affects the genuine relationship the school is attempting to have with the child. It puts staff on edge and they become untrusting.

Remember the saying, "You catch more flies with honey than you do with vinegar"? Make every effort to bring the honey, but it's okay to pull out the vinegar when you need it.

In situations where something makes you angry, go into the school and state your concerns or displeasure in a firm way. Express your points, examples, and feelings about the matter. The school will take you seriously and respect you at the same time. They know that you care and won't hesitate to come back for any other issue. Doing this helps the school system address its weaknesses and, therefore,better serve your child.

If after this step progress is not being made, disperse the vinegar accordingly. It may mean bringing a third party (i.e. advocate, principal, superintendent) in to get some results.

Tip #4
No Communication Chaos

There are times when you are unaware of issues because the school simply can't get in contact with you.

Make sure to:

* Keep your personal information up to date. Ensure that your address, phone, email, and emergency contacts are current.

* Provide background information about personal issues that may affect not only your child's academic performance, but also those which may impact their ability

to properly function in the building; physically, socially or emotionally. For example, you may be going through a divorce, requiring you to elicit help from your high schooler before or after school. This may impact their ability to be on time or stay after school if they need additional help from a teacher. These situations can cause undue stress and deeply impact your child and the school staff. If the school knows about extenuating circumstances (not necessarily the sordid details), there are some resources and services that can be put in place to lessen the burden on the student. The systems work to protect the child from being penalized for contributing factors to their performance which unfortunately reside outside of their control.

* Lastly, return phone calls and emails in a timely fashion, especially if it requires a response.

Tip #5
Learn the Chain of Command

"You don't lead by pointing and telling people some place to go. You lead by going to that place and making a case."

-Ken Kesey-

Schools, just like any other entity, have protocol in how tasks, needs and concerns are addressed. The ideal chain starts with the teacher or school counselor, but if your efforts aren't productive, work your way up:

See Teachers for questions or concerns about the class regarding grading, strengths, weaknesses, missing work, grading, test prep, etc.

See the School Counselor surrounding schedules, grades, mental health, college planning or any other concerns.*

See the Disciplinarian for any issues with a behavioral incident referral or write up, suspension, or safety concern.*

See the Assistant Principal for issues that haven't been satisfied by the teacher, counselor, or disciplinarian.*

See the Principal regarding issues that haven't been satisfied by the teacher, counselor, or disciplinarian in a reasonable time; emergency situations.

Request to meet with the Superintendent concerning issues that have not been satisfied by the school Principal in a reasonable time.

Address the School Board highlighting issues that haven't been satisfied by the school Principal or Superintendent in a reasonable time.

*Not all schools have this position. In this event, continue up the chain.

Note: "Reasonable time" is typically 24-48 hours, unless an emergency (i.e. some type of physical, social or psychological danger).

There are some parents who go straight to the top and that is their prerogative. In those cases, the people at the top are not privy to the situation and do not have a resolution to offer, except to listen to your concerns and get back to you. They will consult with the person the issue should have been taken up with from the beginning. You may find yourself needing to go back to the original source of the concern, thus wasting time.

Remember to Document, Document, Document!

Keep any interactions with the school documented. If there's ever a time you must speak with someone at the school about a concern, they respect and appreciate data. Keep track of times and dates that you made or attempted contact. Having record of emails or notes for this makes you very organized and it is more difficult to argue with a person who has done their due diligence. The school will take you and the situation more seriously.

Tip #6
Identify Resources

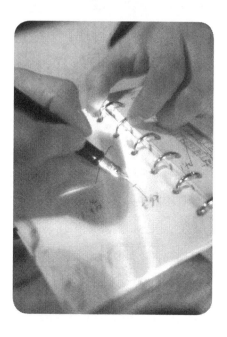

Every school provides access to the ins and outs of the campus and its operations. The information is either sent home or posted online. Information includes:

Student Handbook: Usually available the first day of school, this resource contains the school's stance on dress code, discipline, attendance, bullying, technology, and other policies. They will even name specific staff to contact to address an issue or concern.

Program of Studies (mainly at high school level): This contains all the courses and educational programs the school offers with detailed descriptions (may be combined with the student handbook).

School Newsletter: If a school utilizes this, it's provided either monthly or quarterly and filled with current activities taking place surrounding the student body. (i.e. state testing, field trips, teacher spotlight, sports schedule, awards, etc.).

School Profile (high school only): This form has statistics about the school. The people who typically look for this information are colleges or parents considering transferring their student to the school.

The stats include:

- Grading scale (i.e. A=100-90, B= 89-80, etc.) and credits needed to move to next grade and to graduate

- Advanced Placement (AP) courses offered and average scores on AP test (see Tip #11)
- Honors courses offered (see Tip #11)
- Percentage of students attending 4-year, 2-year, trade school, military, and work (see Tip #13)

Website and Social Media Pages: provides up-to-date school successes, activities, and school closings.

Tip #7
Identify your "Parent by Proxy"

There are legitimate situations where you simply can't maintain physical or verbal contact with the school. You may travel a lot, are a single parent, have a new job (or two jobs), have restrictions on phone use at work, etc. Maybe you're limited in speech , and there's a person who can handle the situation more effectively. Maybe your familiarity with the native language is limited, and a sibling, family member, or friend can engage on your behalf.

It's completely acceptable to appoint another person to represent you as the primary contact. The school is familiar with dealing with grandparents, aunts, uncles, older siblings, etc.

If you are in need of naming another person as your lead point of contact, provide verbal or written authorization to the school about the person who you're allowing to communicate on your behalf (putting them as an emergency contact is essential). Otherwise, the school is not legally allowed to disclose any information to them.

Note: Parents who live separately have situations where an absent parent (rarely involved, negligent, etc.) calls to get information about the child. If the parent is listed on a birth certificate or the emergency card, the school has to disseminate information. Level of involvement in the student's life doesn't matter in the eyes of the law. The only thing that will prevent the release of information is a legal document (i.e. Protection From Abuse (PFA) order) or a custody agreement specifically mandating that there be no contact. The school must have a copy of that document and will ideally contact you know about an attempted communication before speaking to the other parent.

Part II
Parenting and Making use of
Special Services

A solid parental influence creates a more positive and productive school experience. This section details how your parenting style shapes the experience that everyone has with your child(ren). Additionally, it provides tips and programming that can enhance their learning experience.

Tip #8
Remember, You are Your Child's Parent, Not Their Friend

"The greatest gifts you can give your children are the roots of responsibility and the wings of independence."
- Denis Waitley-

There's a saying which quotes "Rules without relationship leads to rebellion." It is important to develop a positive and loving relationship with your child that shows the child is cared for, included and respected in the home. Needless to say, you can have a collaborative relationship with your child, but rules and boundaries are a must.

Your parenting style has a lot to do with the child's temperament and interpersonal skills the school will engage with on a daily basis. The goal is to try to be as balanced as possible. Set boundaries, give your child some latitude to make mistakes, and hold them accountable when they do. In the school setting, this will allow your child to be cooperative and adjust to a level of independence and responsibility.

Sometimes, parents that have a loose parenting style attempt to change to a more productive style and the child actively resists. The student says things like, "you used to do this for me" or "you never cared about that before." They attempt to use guilt as a means to distract or derail you from doing your job of active parenting. Be a parent regardless, do not enable. You are the adult, and they are the child.

You might have to dispense plenty of vinegar here.

Create balance by:

* Not allowing them to work during the week unless they have to (i.e. help pay bills, job-related to their future profession). They have the rest of their life to work. Their "job" right now is to focus on their school work.

* Creating deadlines/boundaries and sticking to them. Say what you mean and mean what you say.

* Encouraging punctuality and regular attendance at school.

* Supporting the school when your child receives a reprimand for clear violations of school policy.

* Not allowing your child to "teacher shop" because they don't like the teacher. Most schools won't allow the student to change teachers unless there

have been on-going issues between the teacher and the child, or it has been determined that the course is an inappropriate placement for the student.

* Inspecting grades and report cards. Take time to read teacher comments and address those that may be concerning with your learner.

* Not doing your child's homework, essays, or filling out forms/applications for them.

Helpful discipline tactics, if they're not doing well in school or at home:

* Take electronics away (even if someone else is paying the bill).

* Remove them from sports and other activities until grades are up to par.

* Totally suspend or restrict privileges (no movies, mall).

* Confiscate car keys if your child is late

to school. Better yet, don't even let them drive to school (my mother is loving this...sigh).

Note: Some teens typically use their electronics into the wee hours on a school night. Sleep researchers say the brain should be resting and winding down at least an hour before bedtime (adults and children). Research also shows that phone activity (texting, talking, playing games, scanning social media), as well as the light from the screens, are very disruptive to the sleep cycle. Decide how you will handle that situation. I collected my kid's phones at night and returned them in the morning. They hated it, but oh well. I was the parent.

Tip #9
Stay In and On Top of Your Child's Business

If I had a dollar for every parent, I heard say "But, she said she was doing good. How did she get these 'F's'?" Know that your good isn't their good. They say they're passing, but remember passing is a "D." That's not doing "good." Stop taking the child's word as bond. Check and verify.

Strategies to raise grades:

* Maintain good attendance at school and class.

* Turn in all assignments.

* Turn in late assignments by the late deadline (schoolwide late policies should be outlined in either the syllabus or student handbook).

* Determine the weight of assignments and make sure your child studies with particular detail for assessments worth

a higher point value (i.e. an in-class assignment may be worth 5 points, a quiz worth 30 points, a test worth 60 points and a book report may be worth 100 points). If the assignment is worth a lot of points, doing well on the assignment could drastically increase the grade. Doing poorly on the assignment could significantly drop the grade. Ask the teacher or school to walk you through how to interpret the grade book.

*   Look at tutoring options. Students will very rarely ask for this resource but it is very important that you, as the active parent, extend it when you know your learner is not meeting your expectations.

*   Get organized (i.e. 3 ring binder, agenda book, folders, etc.).

*   Monitor their grade point average (GPA) every year. The GPA is a number that represents an average of your child's grades. Schools compute a new GPA either each marking period or each year.

(See Tip #14 for more details).

* Talk to the school counselor to strate-gize and increase their average. Ninth graders should do their best to start with a solid GPA. It can be very difficult to raise a low GPA once it's set.

When selecting Courses:

* Try honors or Advanced Placement (AP) courses. If your child is getting an "A" or "B" in a course with no effort, this option will make their transcript more competitive for college and boost their GPA due to the fact that honors and AP classes are weighted more heavily than a typical class. (i.e., if a student gets a "B" in an honors class, it's worth an "A" in a regular class). See Tip #11 for more details on Honors and AP courses.

* Remove honors classes from next year's schedule if your student continuously seems to struggle with content load, pacing, independence or is even failing.

* At the end of each school year, check with the school about next year's schedule. Ask questions about any placement that you do not understand or disagree with concerning his/her grades, etc.

Tip #10
Know All Options and
Special Cases

"Every decision you make - every decision - is not a decision about what to do. It's a decision about Who You Are. When you see this, when you understand it, everything changes. You begin to see life in a new way. All events, occurrences, and situations turn into opportunities to do what you came here to do."

- Neale Donald Walsch-

Documented Accommodations

All public schools must offer the following services free of charge:

504 Plan: A legal and binding document that provides a student with special accommodations in the event of a medical condition that affects learning. Students that have this plan may have a concussion, suffer from persistent migraines, sustained a traumatic brain-injury, irritable bowel syndrome (IBS), or various other short and long-term medical conditions. Students may also be eligible for accommodations during standardized tests such as a state test, the ACT, or the SAT. Most colleges will accept the 504 and provide accommodations through their health services office.

Individualized Education Plan (IEP): A legal and binding plan for a student that requires special educational services to help them be included in, as well as succeed in the classroom. Students range from being in all regular education classes with a teacher monitoring their progress to a smaller setting with the same group of students for the duration of school day. Some students have an IEP and even take honors courses. Students may also be eligible for accommodations during standardized tests such as a state test, the ACT, or the SAT. Most colleges have an office of disabilities to provide support as your child advances through their academic career.

Gifted Individualized Education Plan (GIEP): A legal and binding plan for a student who has a high IQ and requires a more challenging curriculum. Students that receive this service have varying schedules. Programming can include workshops and seminars that take place online and/or outside of the school setting.

English Language Learners (ESL/ELL): A program for students in which English is not their native language and need special support to obtain proficiency. The goal is to test out of the program. Students may be eligible for accommodations during standardized tests such as a state test. They may also take the Test of English as a Foreign Language (TOEFL) exam instead of the ACT or SAT.

Unofficial Accommodations

There are various short-term situations that occur which were not anticipated or an emergency. Once the school is notified, the school counselor and administration can work out a plan to help the student in getting through that particular period.

Absences, tardiness, and medical excuses: Teachers may extend deadlines on an assignment or absences may be excused without an official note for a short period.

You can visit, call the school or send an email to further clarify your individual circumstances.

Family issues/mental health concerns: Make the school aware of any issues that may be causing stress in your family which chance manifesting in school. Examples are a divorce, recent marriage, homelessness, major illness, death, incarceration, loss of a pet, etc. The school counselor can set up counseling services in the school or help you in obtaining outside services. The school can also email your child's teachers letting them know that your child is going through a tough time (nothing specific being disclosed) and to be sensitive to that.

Homelessness: In any event that results in you temporarily moving into a shelter, hotel or with a friend or family member, the school district must make efforts to support families per the McKinney-Vento Act. It is a federal law and districts must make an effort to maintain enrollment in the school, provide transportation (i.e. tokens, cab, van service or alter bus stop) and provide free or reduced lunch. Specific accommodations are made on a case-by-case basis.

Tip #11
Educate Yourself on Available Classes and Programs

Students have options regarding the type of classes they can take. Not all schools have the same programs, but the most common are listed below:

Remedial Classes: These courses allow students to gain a basic foundation before entering a standard course (i.e. taking Pre-Algebra, Algebra IA or IB, before taking Algebra I).

College Prep: A general course that any school offers in the areas of Math, English, Science, and Social Studies.

Honors: A course that prepares students for college-level work. The student must be recommended by a teacher and/or must meet a prerequisite as per the Student Handbook. If your child is not recommended and you feel strongly about it, see the counselor or designee that creates the schedule. In most cases, there is a waiver that you can sign, or you can send an email to an administrator and request a meeting.

Technical and Trade School: Specialized half day or full day programs that allow the student to learn a trade or craft in areas such as Early Childhood Education, Cosmetology, Auto Body & Collision, Construction, and Networking Technology. These programs give students a head start and build self-confidence in regards to post-secondary education options (trade school, 2-year or 4-year programs). Most programs have options for students to earn college credit. Students that are in a special education program can opt to extend their participation in the program beyond graduation.

Advanced Placement (AP): Advanced classes that have more weighted credit than an honors course. Once the class is completed, the student will take a test administered by the College Board (the company that administers the SAT). The scores range from a 1 to 5. If a score of 4 is achieved, often times a college course can be waived. If a student takes a few AP classes and obtains this score, they could shave a few courses from their college roster, which can result in tuition savings or possible early graduation. These play a key role in class rank and/or GPA.

Dual Enrollment: Your child's school works in conjunction with a college to obtain college credit. The student may have the option of taking a college course at a local college or taking the course at school taught by a teacher certified by the college. The school may list the course on the student's transcript (a record of all high school classes and standardized test scores). If not, when applying to college the student can submit the transcript from the college.

Virtual Classes: A computer-based course that a student can take during the school day. These classes are typically reserved for upperclassmen who may have exhausted the curriculum at school and/or want to take a specialized course that most schools don't offer. Honors level courses are available.

Alternative School/Credit Recovery: Your school district may be associated with an alternative school that will accommodate a student with behavioral difficulties or who has a need to recover lost credits so they may graduate on time. These schools typically are smaller in size and provide more individualized attention. Students are placed in the school per administration approval, or a parent can request an application to attend. Space in these environments is very limited.

Cyber/Online School: A computer-based program where the student takes all courses online with a special school. There may be elective classes like health and physical education, where requirements can be satisfied at a local gym or bowling alley. These courses may be taught live, recorded video, or with assistance by email or phone. The student will have access to their teachers, school counselors, and principals. These programs of course recognize IEP's and 504 plans.

Homebound Instruction: A program that accommodates students who cannot attend school for a period of time. A student typically needs to be out a minimum of 6-8 weeks, and a doctor's note is needed to initiate the service. Typically, the school sends a certified teacher to meet with the student (at home or in a public place like a library) in all core subjects and possibly an elective course. Student typically receives one hour a week per subject.

Tip #12
Effectively Transferring to a New School or District

In the event that you have to transfer your child to another school or district, make communication with the current school before withdrawal. The school can collect all the information you need and get it to you before the official withdrawal.

Denial of entry: A school should not be able to deny you registration if you do not have grades. In Pennsylvania, you cannot be denied, however, be sure to research your individual state. If your child attended a private school and money is owed, they are not obligated to release records until the bill is settled.

Grades: Make sure you have updated report cards or transcripts. If you have progress reports for the grading period, they'll be very helpful. Delay in delivery of these documents can result in your student being placed in the wrong courses which can lead to credit reduction or the new school putting the student in a grade level that does not match their most recent educational experience. For example, if no transcript is provided for your junior he/she could be listed as a freshman. Keep a copy of your original report cards and transcript and take them to your meeting with the counselor just in case the file has not been received from the registration office.

Credits and GPA: Every school handles grading differently. Don't assume your child will have the same GPA, grade level, or graduation status at a new school. For senior transfers, attempt to speak with the school counselor to ensure that graduation status is intact. After student records are added to the new school's transcript, check to ensure all courses and grades are accurate. Speak with the counselor to negotiate what options are available if all of your records weren't received or available (i.e. former school didn't send records, the student has been to several schools and marking periods are missing).

State Testing: Many states require a test for students who attend public school to assess their achievement. Some districts in the state make it a requirement to graduate. Your student may be required to take a remedial class or a project-based assessment to prove proficiency.

Part III
Strategies to Effectively Plan for College and other Post-Secondary Options

All of the tips in this section are directly related to information colleges collect on applications. Awareness of this information will allow your student to be more strategic, competitive, and most importantly reduce pre-college expenses.

Visit my website (www.NicholeReneeEnterprises.com) for e-books, personal coaching and/or articles on the college application process.

Tip #13
Decide if College is the
Right Choice

"The two most important days in your life are the day you are born and the day you find out why."
-Mark Twain-

Although the world is pushing the importance of a college education, a 4-year college isn't for everyone. Additionally, every profession doesn't require a 4-year degree. You and your child have to decide if college is for them or not. Have deep and frequent conversations. Listen to your child and hear their heart regarding their career choice. The important thing is that they have a plan. These are your options:

Get a job upon high school graduation: Some students opt to get a job right away. Encourage them to eventually attend trade school or community college at some point to become more marketable or if their plans change in the future.

Enlist in the Military: Students apply during senior year to go into various divisions of the armed forces. Typically, a recruiter makes contact with you and your child through the school, monitors their progress, and prepares them for the transition. The military has many options to provide financial support towards a college degree.

Gap year programs: These programs are for students who would like to take a year off between high school and college. Students may travel to another country, join the Peace Corps, or Teach For America. They may participate in a local program sponsored by the state or government to provide the student with training and classes. Some studies suggest students who participate in these programs enter college with more realistic goals and expectations.

Trade or Technical School: Typically, these are one or two-year programs geared toward achieving a certificate in a field such as cosmetology, auto body, computer networking, or business.

Community College: Students have the option to take one class in a subject that they want to learn, get a certificate in a trade, get an associate's degree in a course of study, or transfer to a 4-year college.

Tip #14
Maintain College Application and Related Deadlines

"One of life's most painful moments comes when we must admit that we didn't do our homework, that we are not prepared."
-Merlin Olsen-

If you're considering applying to college:

* Visit colleges at the top of your child's list. Colleges keep record of the level of interest your child shows in the school

(i.e. filling out contact cards at a college fair, scheduling a personal interview, campus visits, etc.). This can be a game changer when colleges are either filling those last acceptance spaces or if your child's application is borderline on their acceptance requirements but the school wants to give them a chance.

* Maintain a GPA over 3.0 to increase the chances of admission to more selective colleges and scholarships.

* Maintain a GPA over 3.5 to increase the chances of admission to select private and Ivy League schools, as well as heftier scholarship programs.

Pay attention to application deadlines:

* **Rolling Admissions:** Apply at any time of the year until the school has filled its quota.

* **Regular admission:** Schools enforce a specific application deadline after January.

* **Early Decision (ED):** Students may apply early to receive an early acceptance and doing so with the most competitive applicant pool. The decision is binding, and withdrawal of applications to other colleges is required if your student decides to attend. Students should only take this option if the school is their first choice AND financial aid is NOT an issue.

* **Early Admission/Action (EA):** students may submit applications early and receive an early acceptance notification. Students will be applying with a more competitive applicant pool. In contrast to Early Decision, this is not a binding decision.

* **Most colleges have specialized majors** that may have deadlines in September, October, and November. They are very competitive, especially Nursing. Students majoring in Art or Music may have to attend auditions or showcases in addition to submitting an application.

* **Complete the FAFSA (Free Application for Federal Student Aid)** and apply for financial aid regardless of your family's ability to pay. Some scholarships require information from the application. Additionally, if you are looking to get work study or loans from the federal government, this is a requirement. Do not pay anyone to find specific scholarships for you.

* **Attend any workshops** hosted by the school. College Application, Financial Aid, and FAFSA Completion nights are typical programs.

* **There is a national deadline of May 1st** to make a non-refundable deposit to your child's final college choice. You will have to make a general deposit (usually around $200) and at times a dorm deposit (usually around $150-200). Do not allow any school to pressure you to commit earlier than you want to. You may still be able to get in after that date, but run the risk of losing any aid promised by the school.

* **Award letters:** Each college has to provide a letter detailing how many scholarships, grants and loans you have been awarded. Carefully review them and enlist your school counselor to help make the best decision BEFORE making a deposit at the final school of choice.

Tip #15
Recognize the Importance of Extra-Curricular Activities

Extra-curricular activities are crucial to your child's social and cognitive development. They allow your child to learn new things, make new friends, and develop leadership skills. Activities also give them something positive and productive to do with their time after school.

Additionally, participation in these activities can project how your student handles time management—which, in my opinion is the best indicator of success in college.

Examples of activities are:

*   Sports

*   Clubs

*   Part-time jobs

*   Volunteer work at outside organizations (i.e. boy scouts, religious groups, youth group, Sunday school, etc.)

*   Organized activities outside of school

*   Conferences, internships, and summer programs

Your student should pick activities where they have an interest. Having a leadership position (i.e. vice president, secretary, committee member, etc.) is beneficial. Make sure that they don't overload themselves, but maintain a good balance between academics and extra-curriculars.

Tip #16
Explore all Test Prep Options

"If my future were determined just by my performance on a standardized test, I wouldn't be here. I guarantee you that."
-Michelle Obama-

The SAT and ACT are tests that colleges use to assess what your child has learned in high school to determine college readiness. The majority of schools accept the results from either test.

Some things you should know:

* Your child may benefit from taking both tests to determine which is a better fit for his or her personality and test

taking style. If your child chooses to re-test in the Fall, they should take the test they feel most comfortable.

* Your child should not take tests back-to-back (i.e. taking the SAT in May and in June). It takes a few weeks to receive scores and determine where improvements need to be made. If your child struggles with problem solving and correcting their weak points between tests, they run the risk of receiving similar scores on both exams.

* Take the Preliminary SAT (PSAT) or ACT Aspire in 10th and 11th grade (some advanced students take it in earlier years). It is good practice for the SAT as it provides an idea of what to expect from the test. Students typically receive a detailed score report to assist them in getting prepared for the actual test. Additionally, if a high score is achieved, your child can be nominated for a National Merit Scholarship or at least a commendation. Either honor dramatically increases the chance of obtaining

more scholarships and grants that are awarded from the school (these are separate from the traditional scholarships that require applications).

* There are opportunities to take test prep courses through a local testing site. Please consult your school counselor for information for your area.

* In general, the tests are administered on Saturdays across the country. Some schools will administer the test during the school day (in particular the PSAT or the ACT Aspire).

* If your child has an IEP or 504 and needs test accommodations (extra time, extended breaks, etc.), your special education department can submit a request to the testing site. The process takes some time, so plan accordingly. Submission of an application does not guarantee acceptance.

* There is a fee. If your child receives free or reduced lunch or has experienced

some financial hardship, they're eligible for a fee waiver. Your child should alert their counselor, and they'll receive:

- Two (2) waivers for the ACT

- Two waivers (2) for the SAT Reasoning test

- Two waivers (2) for SAT subject tests

- Opportunity to take a free online prep course through the ACT

- Waivers for most, if not all, college application fees. The waivers can amount to hundreds of dollars (Oh joy!).

Other considerations:

* If taking the regular test, make sure your child selects the "Reasoning test NOT the "Subject" test for if the wrong test is selected, a fee will be applied.

* When registering, make sure there are no schedule conflicts with the date. If the date needs to be rescheduled, a fee will be applied.

* Make sure the name listed on testing registration materials are exactly as it appears on the identification your child will use.

* Make sure ID is valid. If the school doesn't print the school year on the ID, preferably take a state ID or passport. Some testing sites may not deem the ID valid without a year listed.

* If the test is missed, a fee will be applied to change it to another date.

If your child is anxious or hasn't had the success they desire with testing, consider applying to a few test optional colleges. Your child may opt to do a writing sample or graded essay instead of submitting standardized test scores. Keep in mind, to be eligible for most merit scholarships (money that a college grants based on academic achievement), the SAT or the ACT score is a must to be considered.

*This information is subject to change, so consult the website for the most detailed and current information. www.collegeboard.org for SAT www.act.org for ACT

**Please consult the NRE website for the article "Should Your Child Take the ACT, SAT or Ditch Them Both" and more detailed information.

Tip #17
Beware of Legal and Discipline Issues

Suspensions, expulsions, and arrests follow your student everywhere they go. Be aware of the following:

Sex, Drugs, and Alcohol: Depending on the school code, any sexual misconduct, the presence of drugs/alcohol, or paraphernalia can result in an expulsion. An expulsion can last for 45 school days to a full year. If your student is suspected of being under the influence, they may be sent for a drug test. Strains of marijuana can stay in your student's system for up to 45 days, and some tests cannot determine if the drug was taken on the day in question or 44 days ago.

Suspensions: Most college applications ask if your student has been suspended. It will require an explanation from your student and the school counselor.

Expulsions: A college can deny any student who's been expelled. If a transfer is attempted to another school to avoid an expulsion, the pending expulsion record goes with your child and will most likely negatively affect admission to the new school. By the way, did you know your child can be expelled for pulling the fire alarm? Be sure to read your school code of conduct closely to familiarize yourself with behavioral expectations.

Arrests and Criminal Convictions: Some colleges ask if there's ever been an arrest There is a movement attempting to eliminate this question from the acceptance process, as a person can be arrested under false pretenses, and/or the arrest does not result in a conviction.

Note: In my experience, I have seen some of the nicest kids with no discipline issues make the mistakes above. Don't assume that only "bad" kids make these mistakes. This note applies to Tip #18 as well.

Tip #18
Know Your Child's Online Persona

Social media is now the way of the world, so pay attention to what your child is doing online. In the world of instant gratification, easy access, and "shock" media, today's child has become desensitized to what is appropriate and what is not appropriate. At times, they cannot make the connection between how their online persona represents them as a person. Many college applications ask about suspensions and expulsions so be aware of the following:

* Colleges have ways to monitor your child on social media. If they see anything inappropriate, this could affect them being accepted to the school. Make sure the email address they use for the school is appropriate as well.

* If your child texts/emails a nude or semi-nude picture of a person, age 17 or under, this is technically considered child pornography. It can result in sus-

pension, expulsion or present legal issues if a parent or school chooses to pursue the issue.

* Cyber-bullying is a big issue for which many schools have a zero tolerance policy. This includes initiations, or hazing. It can result in suspension, expulsion or legal problems if any posts target a particular person(s) and/or are habitual.

Tip #19
Being a Great Athlete Does Not Equal a Scholarship

Many student-athletes have dreams that they'll play college or professional sports. Moreover, they think they're good enough to get a scholarship. Their likelihood or talent has to be determined by their stats, scouts, and various other factors out of their control. For example, the"full ride"

scholarships that students go for are only provided through Division I or II colleges.

Have your child complete applications for the school they desire to attend. Don't wait for a scout or coach to 'walk the application' through unless you're told to do so.

Your student should create an account in the NCAA Eligibility Center (www.eligibilitycenter.org) during the beginning of their junior year:

* There they can upload their current classes and courses from their transcript.

* There is a fee. If your child receives free or reduced lunch or has experienced some financial hardship, they are eligible for a fee waiver. Your child should alert their counselor, and they'll submit it online.

* Your child must have a minimum of 2.3 GPA in their "core" classes. Examples of

core classes are Math, English, Social Studies, Science, and Foreign Languages.

* It's highly recommended to visit the site in 10th grade to see what the NCAA approved classes are. Check the site to ensure the core classes your child is taking are on the NCAA requirement list.

* The eligibility center's GPA isn't the same as your child's school. Once the classes and grades are placed in the system, the site will convert it to their GPA.

*This information is subject to change, so consult the website for the most detailed and current information. www.eligibilitycenter.org

Tip #20
Effectively Deal with
"Senioritis"

"The good news is that the bad news can be turned
into good news when you change your attitude."
-Robert H. Schuller-

Every senior, no matter how great of a student, falls prey to the curse of "senioritis." Many assumptions are made regarding graduation. Kids fall into a false sense of security that they'll pass. They become very lax with their attendance, skip assignments or finals, and cruise through the last marking period. They're tired, stressed, and overwhelmed, and don't feel like meeting their responsibilities. The chances of them slacking off and allowing grades to decline can be high.

Again, don't take them at their word. Check and verify for this is the most crucial time of follow-up with the school. Make sure you:

* Contact the school counselor to see

progress in grades, attendance and other areas of concern.

*   Check with the counselor to see which classes are required for graduation.

*   Don't allow your child to schedule classes they have a history of failing (unless it is a requirement). If your child has a history of failing classes, it's likely they will fail some senior courses. Stay in contact with school regularly to avoid surprises.

*   Schools typically do not drop courses after the first quarter unless there's a dire reason. Make sure that students are not going to overwhelm themselves their senior year by taking too many honors or AP classes that they will then ask to be removed from later.

*   Make sure your child avoids getting any "F's" in a class that is not required for graduation. The "F" will lower their final grade point average. Additionally, it's very common to have to request a

transcript in the future for a job or college transfer and any failure, regardless of what the class is, doesn't look good.

* Check online or with teachers to ensure that your child doesn't have an unexpected grade drop during the last marking period. Some may still pass their classes, but may get a "D" in a course that should have resulted in a "B" or "C."

* Make sure all other graduation requirements have been satisfied (i.e. graduation project, senior paper, etc.).

* Colleges will ask for final transcripts. If your child made a major decline, the school has the option of revoking their acceptance. It's not an everyday occurrence, but it does happen.

* Make arrangements for final transcripts to be sent to the college. These aren't available until after graduation. Not doing this will delay registration for classes and moving on campus.

Closing Thoughts

"No one lives long enough to learn everything they need to learn starting from scratch. To be successful, we absolutely, positively have to find people who have already paid the price to learn the things that we need to learn to achieve our goals."

-Brian Tracy-

There are tons of books on the subject of college planning, parenting and other various topics related to secondary schools (middle, junior and high school). There aren't many books that provide detailed information on the inner workings of the school, especially from the perspective of someone currently working in the field.

The schools want to work with you. They do! It doesn't have to be a scary, stressful or "us versus them" experience. You can make your experience more pleasurable by working in harmony with your school or effectively taking an aggressive stance to advocate for your child. Either way, you will be taking advantage of all of the options your child qualifies for and setting them up for success.

For this book, I pulled from my over eighteen years of experience serving as a school counselor and provided you with every essential tip that I felt would help you better navigate the school system. Once you have a grasp on the operating functions of a school, the role your parenting style plays in the process, and the services, resources and options available you can better strategize for your child's postsecondary planning.

Over the years, it has been a painful experience to see a parent struggling with an issue due to lack of knowledge.

I don't want you to be the parent of the 10th grader who could have benefitted from special education, 504 or gifted services at an earlier time. I don't want you to be the parent of the talented senior that left thousands of dollars on the table because they didn't take advantage of a more challenging curriculum, extracurricular activities or important application deadlines. I want you to be the parent that knows you're not perfect but took advantage of as many opportunities as you could, enjoyed an on-time graduation, got your child on a quicker path to their dreams—and kept some money in your pocket in the process.

It is my hope that you enjoyed this book and was able to come away with a clearer perspective of the inner-workings of the secondary school system, as well as, walk away with more tools for your toolkit. There is a saying that quotes, 'If you aren't at the table you will definitely be on the menu.' By reading this book, you have reserved your seat at the table and staked your claim. Be more confident and educated as you interact with your child's school. Make yourself known!

Wishing you the best,
Nichole Renee

Need a few more college planning tips?

Subscribe to my mailing list and get my FREE ebook!

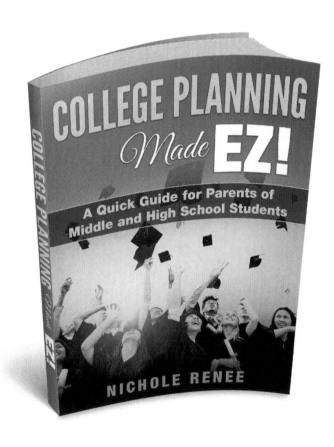

Need Assistance!

As technology and the time changes, so will some of the systems discussed in this book. You need an ally in the field to keep you abreast of the changes, fight for you and get you to the finish line. You need someone who can get you through the college application process and help you keep some money in your pocket. Allow me to coach you through the process! Visit my website and get your
FREE 20-minute consultation today!

For more information about my workshops, webinars and coaching packages visit my blog or resource page at:

www.NicholeReneeEnterprises.com

NICHOLE RENEE
Enterprises

Communicate · Educate · Liberate

BONUS SECTION

Share this with your Middle, Ninth and Tenth Graders and give them a head start!

MIDDLE SCHOOL

Fall and Spring

* Start having more strategic conversations about your dreams and career goals. Your plans may change but it's always good to explore.
* If you are bored in class and/or getting A's and B's with no problem, consider taking some advanced or honors level classes. This will prepare you for advanced classes in high school.
* If your plan is to go into a heavy math or science field, you should take Algebra I in the 7th or 8th grade in order to take Calculus and Physics by senior year.
* Get a library card if you don't have one and brush up on your reading.
* Get involved in extra-curricular activities. This will allow you to make new friends, discover new interests and have something positive and productive to do after school.
* Do some volunteer work or work a summer camp. Get involved at your local YMCA.

* Talk to your parents about getting involved in PTA

Summer Plans

* If there is a summer reading requirement, make sure all is completed. The schools that require them make it a major assignment for the first quarter/trimester of school. Not doing well can dramatically affect the final grade.

GRADE NINE

* If there is a summer reading require-ment, make sure all is completed.

* Make an appointment with your coun-selor.

* Discuss your academic/career plans and personal and academic strengths.

* Visit the your School Counselor and/or College Career Center.

* Learn about the various extracurricular activities in school and join one.

* Maintain strong grades this year. Col-leges begin looking at grades in fresh-man year!

* Seek help if you are having trouble with a class. Discuss with your teacher so they can give you recommendations.

* Make a decision if you want to go to college, attend a technical school, the armed services or plan to work after you graduate.

Spring

* Meet with your counselor to talk about your grades and courses for the next year, Base the discussion off of your graduation goals and career interests.
* If you are considering attending a vocational or technical school, understand that you are preparing for a career in that area after high school.
* Considering college? Two years of the same world language is required at most four-year colleges/universities.
* Attend college fairs at your school or in your area.
* Identify subjects that you enjoy and have a strength in. Explore careers associated with that subject.
* Talk to your counselor about summer Enrichment programs (around February).
* Attendance is important to success in school. Go to school every day and on time!

Summer Plans

* Take time to read, find ways to write, and review math worksheets to maintain these skills.
* Log onto College Board (www.collegboard.com) and do practice questions for the PSAT that you will take in the fall.

GRADE TEN

Fall

* If there is a summer reading require-ment, make sure all is completed.
* Continue your participation in school activities, community involvement and other extracurricular activities.
* You now know the school environment. Take a huge leap in accepting responsi-bility and wise choices this year --aca-demically and socially.
* Set goals for yourself; you might have to make new friends who have similar goals as yours in order to stay focused on school.
* Take the PSAT, a practice test for the SAT, and take it seriously so that you can use it to begin the college search process.
* Visit the college career center (if you have one).
* Review your grades on your transcript with your counselor and set goals to improve your GPA.
* Understand your class rank which can

affect the type of college that will admit you.

* Attend a local or Regional College Career Fair.
* Complete the task list on Collegeboard to explore careers.
* Find a place to do volunteer work.
* Add your school activities for a resume senior year.

Spring

* Plan next year's courses to reflect your interests, school progress, and emerging career plans.
* Consider taking SAT Subject tests in your major courses if you are considering selective colleges and if you are getting A's and B's in classes.
* Challenge yourself with Honors or Advanced Placement courses, if you are recommended.
* Advanced Placement courses are high school courses that you can get college credit after taking the AP test and receive a score of 3, 4 or 5.

* Attend an AP Potential day and evening Programs if you are recommended (all schools do not have this).
* Create a College Board account and review the questions that you answered incorrectly on the PSAT to improve SAT scores.
* Review your credits to make sure that you are on task to graduate on time.
* Make sure that you are maintaining good relationships with your teachers who you will need to ask for recommendations in your senior year.
* Attendance is important to college admissions and to future employers.

Summer

* Consider summer enrichment programs on college campuses.
* Volunteer work is something that you can do in areas where you are considering a future career.
* Summer reading can improve your vocabulary.
* Consider a part-time job.

* If you don't have an email create one. Colleges will use it to contact you in the fall.
* Consider an SAT or PSAT prep program at your school or local community college.